D0160383

Dear Reader:

Have you ever needed to have a good joke on hand to get out of a tough situation or maybe just to lighten a gloomy moment?

Well, here is a joke book with all the best cat-and-dog jokes you could ever want to know. Impress all your pet-owning friends with your amazing knowledge. You can learn such important things as

☞ how to spell "mousetrap" in three letters: CAT.

☞ what kind of flower Lassie likes: collie flower

☞ what kind of cat doesn't say meow: catfish

☞ what's green and barks: a pup tent

And many other purr-fectly silly things.

Both the author and illustrator of this book have produced many other books. Charles Keller (author) has done more than thirty joke-and-riddle books. Robert Quackenbush has illustrated more than one hundred and fifty books.

Choose your favorite joke! And remember it for when you need it most!

Sincerely,

Elizabeth Isele
Executive Editor
Weekly Reader Books

Weekly Reader Book Club Presents

It's Raining Cats and Dogs
Cat and Dog Jokes

Compiled by Charles Keller
Illustrated by Robert Quackenbush

PIPPIN PRESS
New York

For Nicole and Leigh

This book is a presentation of Weekly Reader Books. Weekly Reader Books offers book clubs for children from preschool through high school. For further information write to: **Weekly Reader Books,** 4343 Equity Drive, Columbus, Ohio 43228.

Published by arrangement with Pippin Press. Weekly Reader is a federally registered trademark of Field Publications.

Text copyright © 1988 by Charles Keller
Illustrations copyright © 1988 by Robert Quackenbush
All rights reserved. No part of this book may be reproduced in any form, or by any means, except for the inclusion of brief quotations in a review, without permission in writing from the publisher.

Published by Pippin Press, New York

Printed in the United States of America   .J

10 9 8 7 6 5 4 3 2

Library of Congress Cataloging-in-Publication Data

Keller, Charles.
   It's raining cats and dogs.

   Summary: A collection of jokes about cats and dogs.
Example: What's the worst weather for rats and mice?
When it's raining cats and dogs.
      1. Cats—Juvenile humor.   2. Dogs—Juvenile humor.
3. Wit and humor, Juvenile.   [1. Cats—Wit and humor.
2. Dogs—Wit and humor.   3. Jokes]   I. Quackenbush,
Robert M., ill.   II.Title.
PN6231.C23K45 1988 818′.5402 88-12421
ISBN 0-945912-01-3

What's the worst weather for rats and mice?
When it's raining cats and dogs.

Why is a hot dog the noblest of all dogs?
Because it feeds the hand that bites it.

Why did the boy refuse to buy a hot dog?
He thought it was a stolen poodle.

When is it bad luck for a black cat to follow you?
When you're a mouse.

What kind of cat should you never play games with?
A cheetah.

Why don't dogs like to travel in airplanes?
Because they suffer from jet wag.

What's purple and bites?
A grape dane.

What do you call a police dog?
A copper spaniel.

What's the best thing for a dog with a fever?
Mustard. It's the best thing for a hot dog.

What kind of dog has money?
A bloodhound. It's always picking up scents.

What sickness does a dog get?
Arf-ritis.

How can you tell if a cat burglar has been in your house?
Your cat is missing.

What do you get when you cross a chicken with a poodle?
Pooched eggs.

What do you call an All-American canine?
A yankee poodle.

What do puppies and trains have in common?
They both chew, chew, chew.

What did the man say when his cat was run over by a steamroller?
Nothing. He just stood there with a long puss.

What do you call a flea that lives on a French poodle?
A Paris-ite.

What is a dog's favorite car?
A Hounda.

How do cats train at the Red Cross?
They give mouse-to-mouse resuscitation.

What do you call a dog who plays baseball?
A catcher's mutt.

What do you call a cat's I.O.U.?
Pussy will-ow.

What's a puppy's favorite soda?
Pupsi Cola.

What do you get when you cross a hyena and a hot dog?
Hot cross puns.

What must you know before you can teach a dog tricks?
More than the dog.

What do you get when you cross a German Shepherd with a clock?
A watch dog.

How is cat food sold?
At so much purr can.

What do you get when you cross a kitten with an apartment?
A house cat.

What Confederate general was a dog during the Civil War?
Robert E. Flea.

What happens when a cat swallows a fish?
He gets findigestion.

What's it called when it rains cats?
A great downpurr.

How are dog catchers paid?
By the pound.

When is a black dog not a black dog?
When it's a grayhound.

Why did the lazy boy buy a great big dog?
So he wouldn't have to bend down to pet it.

Why is Lassie like a comet?
They are both stars with tails.

If a dog has fleas, what does a sheep have?
Fleece.

What does a cat rest his head on when he goes to sleep?
A cat-er-pillar.

What do you get when you cross a dachshund and a zebra?
Striped sausages.

What's the difference between a coyote and a flea?
One howls on the prairie and the other prowls on the hairy.

What dog do you find at the United Nations.
A diplo-mutt.

What has eight arms and drinks milk?
An octopussy.

How can you tell one type of cat from another?
By referring to a cat-a-logue.

What do you get when you cross a pointer with a setter?
A pointsettia.

How do we know that cats always land on their fathers?
Because cats always land on their paws.

How do you get milk from a cat?
Steal its saucer.

What prize do actor cats win?
The A-cat-emy Award.

What movie scares dogs."
"The Twilight Bone."

What name do you call a wiener dog?
Frank.

What is an octopus?
A cat that lost one of its lives.

What do you call a dog who sleeps all the time?
A schnoozer.

What's green and barks?
A pup tent.

What does a five-hundred pound mouse say?
"Here, kitty, kitty."

What did the cat see when it saw the mouse crying?
Mouse-ke-tears.

What did the frankfurter say to the dog who bit it?
"It's a dog-eat-dog world."

How did the convict get away from the bloodhound?
He threw a penny in the river and it followed the wrong cent.

What does a cat sing at night in space?
"O Solar Meow."

Why is a cheap dog a poor watchdog?
Because bargain dogs don't bite.

What happened to the dog who swallowed a watch?
He got a lot of ticks.

Why does a cat have fur?
If he didn't, he'd be a little bare.

Why did the dog run away from home?
Doggone if I know.

What are a dog's clothes made of?
Mutt-erial.

Why did the vet operate on the dog?
Because a stitch in time saves canine.

What's the most dangerous job in Transylvania?
A dog catcher on nights when the moon is full.

What do you get when you cross an owl with a cat?
An owly cat.

Why did the boy feed his cat pennies?
He heard you should put some money in the kitty.

Why did Snoopy quit the comic strip?
He got tired of working for peanuts.

How do they keep a barking dog quiet?
With hush puppies.

Why did the cat want the package marked C.O.D.?
It sounded fishy to him.

What's the difference between a whale hunter and a happy dog?
One tags his whale, the other wags his tail.

What dog is the most expensive?
A deer hound.

What's the difference between a dog and a flea?
A dog can have fleas, but a flea can't have dogs.

If every dog has his day, what does a dog with a broken tail have?
A weak end.

What kind of cats live in churches?
Holy cats.

What's the difference between a dog and a gossip?
One has a wagging tail and the other a wagging tongue.

What do you call a tired police dog?
A-resting.

What magazine do cats read?
Good Mousekeeping.

What do you call a happy Lassie?
A jolly collie.

When do cats have eight legs?
When there are two of them.

What is Garfield the Cat's middle name?
The.

Why does a cat have a fur coat?
Because he'd look silly in a raincoat.

Where do cats vacation in Florida?
Meowmi Beach.

What cat jumps three feet every five seconds?
One with hiccups.

What kind of cat lives in a backyard?
A clothes lion.

What city is very dangerous for cats?
Curious-city.

What goes "Meow" and has two wheels?"
A cat on a motorcycle.

Why did the man call his dog "Peeve"?
So he could have a pet peeve.

When is a dog like a fighter?
When he's a boxer.

What kind of shoes do mice wear to get away from cats?
Squeakers.

What's white, fluffy and barks?
Pupcorn.

What kind of flower does Lassie like?
A collie flower.

How can you tell the difference between a dogwood tree and a dog?
Listen to their barks.

What do you get when you cross an octopus with a cat?
I don't know, but it would have eight arms and nine lives.

What does a dog have on top of his house?
A woof.

How many paws do dogs and cats have?
One pa and one ma.

What do you call a sleepy bulldog?
A bulldozer.

What do rich cats drive?
Cat-illacs.

What do you get when you cross a dog and a cat?
An animal that chases itself.

What is dog candy called?
Bone-bons.

What did the fish say to the cat?
"Sorry, I can't stay for dinner."

What do you call it when 1,000 cats and dogs are sent to the pound?
A doggone cat-astrophe.

Why did the dog cross the street twice?
Because he was a double-crosser.

When is a storyteller like a happy dog?
When his tale is moving.

Why are dogs experts on trees?
So they won't bark up the wrong one.

Why couldn't the cat catch the mouse running out of the stove?
It was out of his range.

What do you get when you cross a frog with a dog?
A croaker spaniel.

What do you get when you cross a hyena and a collie?
A dog that laughs through Lassie movies.

Why are there no psychiatrists for dogs?
Because dogs are not allowed on couches.

Why did the girl stop the cat from eating her stocking?
She didn't want a sock in her puss.

What does a dog get when it graduates from school?
A pet-igree.

What dog keeps the best time?
A watch dog.

What happened to the cat that swallowed a ball of string?
She had mittens.

How can you tell when you have a slow dog?
He brings you yesterday's paper.

What kind of market does a dog hate?
A flea market.

How do you spell mousetrap in three letters?
C-A-T.

What time of year does a cat pounce on a
mouse?
Springtime.

Why didn't the girl get a kitten for her baby
brother?
Because no one would trade with her.

Who has more lives than a cat's nine lives?
Frogs. They croak every night.

Why does a dog wear more clothes in summer than in winter?
In winter it wears a coat, but in summer it wears a coat and pants, too.

What cat doesn't say meow?
A catfish.

Why couldn't the dog catch his tail?
It's hard to make ends meet these days.

How did the cat know the mouse was in the refrigerator?
He saw his footprints in the cheesecake.

Are cats rich?
No, most are purr.

What's the worst weather for rats and mice?
When it's raining cats and dogs.